# Body And Raiment

# BODY AND RAIMENT
BY EUNICE TIETJENS

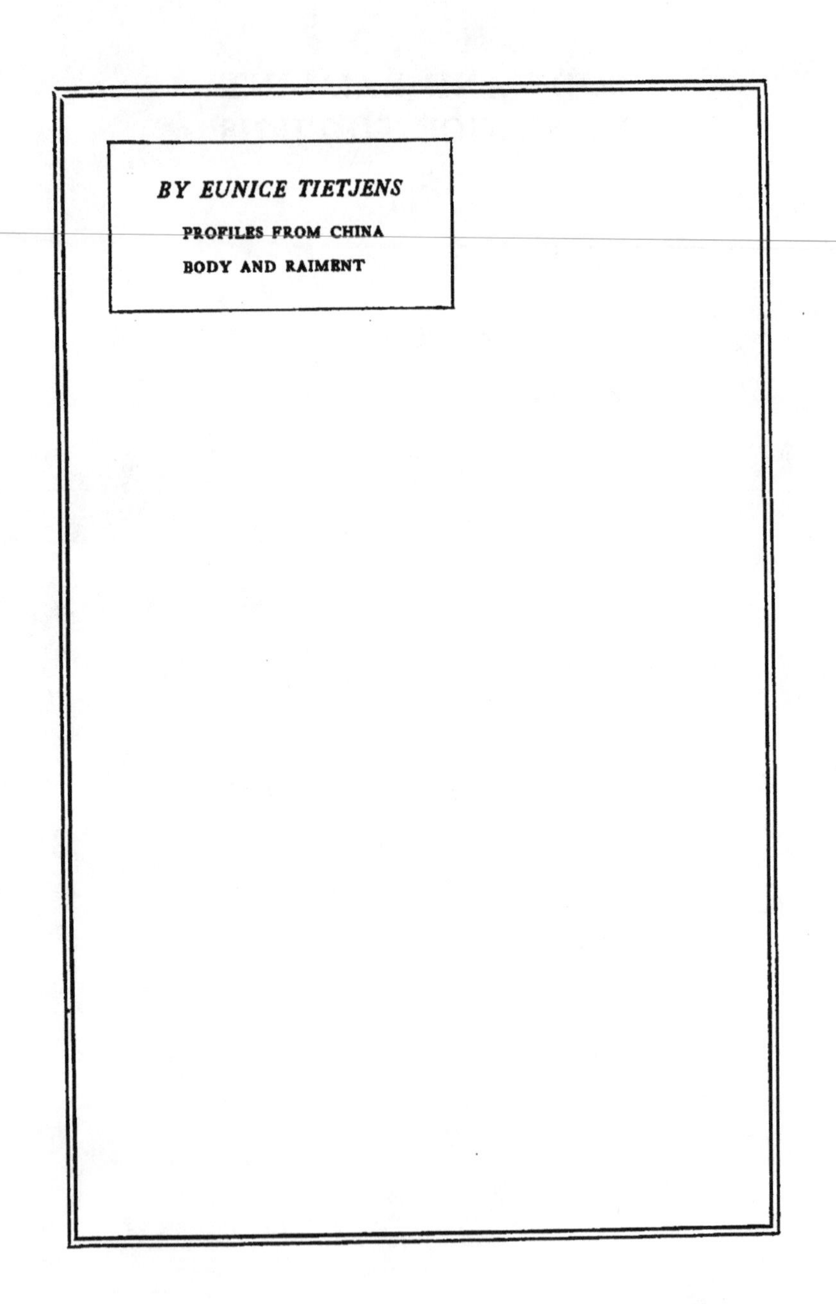

*BY EUNICE TIETJENS*

PROFILES FROM CHINA

BODY AND RAIMENT

# BODY AND RAIMENT
## BY EUNICE TIETJENS

NEW YORK: ALFRED · A · KNOPF
MCMXIX

PRINTED IN THE UNITED STATES OF AMERICA

To Janet

My Daughter and My Delight

# CONTENTS

*PROEM*



*BODY AND RAIMENT*

*TRANSLATIONS AND RENDERINGS INTO ENGLISH VERSE*

# Proem

## A Plaint of Complexity

I have too many selves to know the one.
In too complex a schooling was I bred,
Child of too many cities, who have gone
Down all bright cross-roads of the world's desires,
And at too many altars bowed my head
To light too many fires.

One polished self I have, she who can sit
Familiarly at tea with the marquise
And play the exquisite
In silken rustle lined with etiquette,
Chatting in French, Italian, what you please,
Of this and that . . .
Who sings now at La Scala, what's the gown
Fortuni's planned for "La Louise,"
Or what *Les Jeunes* are at in London town.
She can look out
At dusk across Lung' Arno, sigh a bit,
And speak with shadowy feeling of the rout
This brute modernity has made
Of Beauty and of Art;
And sigh with just the proper shade
Of scorn for Guido Reni, just the "Ah!"
For the squeezed martyrs of El Greco.

And I've a modern, rather mannish self
Lives gladly in Chicago.
She believes
That woman should come down from off her shelf

Of calm dependence on the male
And labor for her living.
She likes men,
And equal comradeship, and giving
As much as she receives.
She likes discussions lasting half the night,
Lit up with wit and cigarettes,
Of art, religion, politics and sex,
Science and prostitution. She thinks art
Deals first of all with life, and likes to write
Poems of drug clerks and machinery.
She's very independent—and at heart
A little lonely . . .

I've a horrid self,
A sort of snob, who's travelled here and there
And drags in references by the hair
To steamship lines, and hotels in Hong Kong,
The temple roofs of Nikko, and the song
Of the Pope's Nightingale.
She always speaks,
In passing, of the great men whom she knows,
And leaves a trail
Of half impressed but irritated foes.
My other selves dislike her, but we can't
Get rid of her at certain times and places,
And there are faces
That wake her in me.

I've a self compound of strange, wild things,
Of solitude, and mud, and savagery;

Loves mountain tops and deserts
And the wings
Of great hawks beating black against the sky.
Would love a man to beat her. . . .

I've a self might almost be a nun,
So she loves peace, prim gardens in the sun
Where shadows shift at evening,
Hands at rest,
And the clear lack of questions in her breast.

And deeper yet there is my mother self,
Something not so much I as womankind,
That surges upward from a blind
Immeasurable past.
A little laughing daughter, a cool child
Sudden and lovely as a wild
Young wood-thing, she has somehow caught
And holds half unbelieving. She has wrought
Love-bands to hold her fast
Of courage, tenderness and truth,
And memories of her own white youth,
The best I am, or can be.
This self stands
When others come and go, and in her hands
Are balm for wounds and quiet for distractions,
And she's the deepest source of all my actions.

But I've another self she does not touch,
A self I live in much, and overmuch

These latter years.
A self who stands apart from outward things,
From pleasure and from tears,
And all the little things I say and do.
She feels that action traps her, and she swings
Sheer out of life sometimes, and loses sense
Of boundaries and of impotence.
I think she touches something, and her eyes
Grope, almost seeing, through the veil
Towards the eternal beauty in the skies
And the last loveliness that cannot fail.

But what she sees in her far spirit world,
Or what the center is
Of all this whirl of crowding I's,
I cannot tell you—only this:
That I've too many selves to know the one;
In too complex a schooling was I bred,
Child of too many cities, who have gone
Down all bright cross-roads of the world's desires,
And at too many altars bowed my head
To light too many fires.

# Body and Raiment

# The Bacchante to her Babe

*Scherzo*

Come, Sprite, and dance! The sun is up,
The wind runs laughing down the sky
That brims with morning like a cup;
Sprite, we must race him,
We must chase him
You and I!
And skim across the fuzzy heather,
You and joy and I together
Whirling by!

You merry little roll of fat!
Made warm to kiss, and smooth to pat,
And round to toy with, like a cub,
To put one's nozzle in and rub
And breathe you in like breath of kine,
Like juice of vine,
That sets my morning heart a-tingling,
Dancing, jingling,
All the glad abandon mingling
Of wind and wine!

Sprite, you are love, and you are joy,
A happiness, a dream, a toy,
A god to laugh with,
Love to chaff with,
The sun come down in tangled gold,
The moon to kiss and spring to hold.

There was a time once, long ago,
Long, oh, long since . . . I scarcely know;
Almost I had forgot . . .
There was a time when you were not,
You merry sprite, save as a strain,
The strange dull pain
Of green buds swelling
In warm straight dwelling
That must burst to the April rain.
A little heavy I was then
And dull, and glad to rest. And when
The travail came
In searing flame . . .
But, sprite, that was so long ago!
A century! I scarcely know.
Almost I had forgot
When you were not.

So, little sprite, come dance with me!
The sun is up, the wind is free!
Come now and trip it,
Romp and skip it;
Earth is young and so are we.
Sprite, you and I will dance together
On the heather,
Glad with all the procreant earth,
With all the fruitage of the trees,
And golden pollen on the breeze;
With plants that bring the grain to birth,
With beast and bird,
Feathered and furred,

With youth and hope and life and love
And joy thereof,
While we are part of all, we two,
For my glad burgeoning in you!

So, merry little roll of fat,
Made warm to kiss and smooth to pat
And round to toy with, like a cub,
To put one's nozzle in and rub;
My god to laugh with,
Love to chaff with,
Come and dance beneath the sky
You and I!
Look out with those round wondering eyes,
And squirm, and gurgle—and grow wise!

## Psalm to My Belovéd

Lo, I have opened unto you the wide gates of my being,
And like a tide you have flowed into me.
The innermost recesses of my spirit are full of you, and all the channels of my soul are grown sweet with your presence.
For you have brought me peace;
The peace of great tranquil waters, and the quiet of the summer sea.
Your hands are filled with peace as the noon-tide is filled with light; about your head is bound the eternal quiet of the stars, and in your heart dwells the calm miracle of twilight.
I am utterly content.
In all my spirit is no ripple of unrest.
For I have opened unto you the wide gates of my being
And like a tide you have flowed into me.

## A Song of Loneliness

The silver night is faint with beauty;
The iris shimmer in the moon;
Soft as the words of love remembered
The night winds croon.

No tremor shakes the moon in heaven;
The gleaming iris feel no smart,
And nothing aches in all this beauty
Except my heart.

## To a Lost Friend

Across the tide of years you come to me,
You whom I knew so long ago.
A poignant letter kept half carelessly,
A faded likeness, dull and gray to see . . .
And now I know.

Strange that I knew not then—that when you stood
In warm, sweet flesh beneath my hand,
Your soul tumultuous as a spring-time flood
And life's new wonder pulsing in your blood,
I could not understand.

I could not see your soul like thin red fire
Flash downward to my gaze,
Nor guess the strange, half understood desire,
The tumult and the question and the ire
Of those far days.

It is too late now. You have dropped away
In formless silence from my ken
And youth's high hopes turn backward to decay.
Yet oh, my heart were very fain today
To love you then!

## The Drug Clerk

The drug clerk stands behind the counter,
Young and dapper, debonair . . .

Before him burn the great unwinking lights,
The hectic stars of city nights,
Red as hell's pit, green as a mermaid's hair.
A queer half acrid smell is in the air.
Behind him on the shelves in ordered rows
With strange abbreviated names
Dwell half the facts of life. That young man knows
Bottled and boxed and powdered here
Dumb tragedies, deceptions, secret shames,
And comedy, and fear.

Sleep slumbers here, like a great quiet sea
Shrunk to this bottle's compass, sleep that brings
Sweet respite from the teeth of pain
To those poor tossing things
That the white nurses watch so thoughtfully.
And here again
Dwell the shy souls of Maytime flowers
That shall make sweeter still those poignant hours
When wide-eyed youth looks on the face of love.
And, for those others who have found too late
The bitter fruit thereof,
Here are cosmetics, powders, paints—the arts
That hunted women use to hunt again
With scented flesh for bait.
And here is comfort for the hearts

Of sucking babes in their first teething pain.
Here dwells the substance of huge fervid dreams,
Fantastic, many-colored, shot with gleams
Of ecstasy and madness, that shall come
To some pale twitching sleeper in a bunk.
And here is courage, cheaply bought
To cure a sick blue funk,
And dearly paid for in the final sum.
Here in this powdered fly is caught
Desire more ravishing than Tarquin's, rape
And bloody-handed murder. And at last
When the one weary hope is past
Here is the sole escape,
The little postern in the house of breath
Where pallid fugitives keep tryst with death.

All this the drug clerk knows, and there he stands,
Young and dapper, debonair . . .
He rests a pair of slender hands,
Much manicured, upon the counter there
And speaks: "No, we don't carry no pomade.
We only cater to the high-class trade."

## Song

In the little hills of Tryon
My love is hid away,
Fed on rain and beauty
All the April day.

Oh, love is big as doomsday
And stronger than the sea,
Yet the little hills of Tryon
Can hide my love from me.

## The Great Man

I cannot always feel his greatness.
Sometimes he walks beside me, step by step,
And paces slowly in the ways—
The simple, wingless ways
That my thought treads. He gossips with me then
And finds it good;
Not as an eagle might, his great wings folded, be content
To walk a little, knowing it his choice,
But as a simple man,
My friend.
And I forget.

Then suddenly a call floats down
From the clear airy spaces,
The great, keen lonely heights of being.
Then he who was my comrade hears the call
And rises from my side, and soars,
Deep-chanting to the heights.
Then I remember.
And my upward gaze goes with him, and I see
Far off against the sky
The glint of golden sunlight on his wings.

## Completion

My heart has fed today.
My heart, like hind at play,
Has grazed in fields of love, and washed in streams
Of quick, imperishable dreams.

In moth-white beauty shimmering,
Lovely as birches in the moon glimmering,
From coigns of sleep my eyes
Saw dawn and love arise.

And like a bird at rest,
Steady in a swinging nest,
My heart at peace lay gloriously
While wings of ecstasy
Beat round me and above.

I am fulfilled of love.

## Defeat

I have seen him, and his hand
Has that slow gesture still.

My tutored heart
That had gone quietly these many months,
And happily, securely, beat its way
Glad to be free of the old instancy—
My heart betrayed me.
Cowardly it stopped;
And then it leaped; and the old Panic hoofbeats thundered in my ears.

Oh, is there then no peace for me
When old love will not die?
And shall I conquer all things,
Thrusting up, through the intolerable pain of growth,
Until my soul
Leaps wingéd to the sunset's rim,
Only at last to break my self on love
And fall a-trembling like an aching girl
Because he has a beautiful slow hand?

## To My Friend, Grown Famous

(E. L. M.)

The mail has come from home,—
From home that still remembers,—to Japan.
My tiny maid, as faultless as a fan,
Bows in the doorway. " Honorable letters,"
She says, " have kindly come."
And smiles, knowing the fetters
That bind me still.

And all my mail today is full of you.
"His name," says one, "is sounding still and sounding."
And someone else, "It is astounding;
I never knew the public chatter worse.
Nineteen editions for a book of verse!"
And all the printed pages glitter, too,
With you;
With your stark vision and cold fire,
Your singing truth, your vehement desire
To cut through lies to life.
These move behind the printed echoes here,
The paper strife,
The scurry of small pens about your name,
Measuring, praising, blaming by the same
Tight rule of thumb that makes their own
Inadequacy known.
And as I read a phrase leaps clear
From your own letter: "I am tired," you say,
"Of men who talk and talk and dare not live,

But take their orgasms in speech!"
Yes, that would be your way
To take the critics. It is you who give,
Not they;
And safe beyond their reach
Huge, careless, Rabelaisian, you pass by,
Watching their squirming with amuséd eye.

Here as I sit,
My paper house-side slid away
And all my chamber open to the rain,
I feel a haunting, exquisite
Grey shadow of a pain.
Beauty has part in it, and loneliness,
And the far call of home—and thoughts of you
In the rain of spring.
Here in this land of frozen loveliness,
Of artistry complete, where each small thing
Minutely, preciously, is perfect,
I have grown hungry for the sight of you
Who are not perfect,
Who are big and free
And largely vulgar like the peasantry,
And full of sorrows for mankind.
I cannot find
Your spirit in this land. The little tree
Tortured and dwarfed—oh! beautiful I know
In the grey slanting rain,
But tortured even so—
The little pine tree in my garden close
Is symbol of the soul that grows

Within this patient cult of loveliness.
You would not understand,
Would care far less
For the pale, silvered shadows of this land
That make it dear to me.
Yet when I see
Your clear handwriting march across the page,
And your brave spirit of a tonic age
Blow sharp across the spring
I smother here a little;
This conscious beauty is so light, so brittle,
So frail a thing!

But you are free! "Go out," your letter says,
"Go drink life to the lees.
See the round world! Watch where Lord Buddha sits
Beneath the tree; and see where Jesus walked
And talked.
See where Aspasia and Pericles
Have visited together, and where Socrates
Leaned on the wall. . . .
Go out, my friend, and see—
And then come back and tell it all to me!"

That, too, is like you; "Tell it all to me."
I feel your spirit searching hungrily
Each human being for the stuff of life,
The sharp blue flame below the smoke,
The authentic cry
That all our mouthing cannot choke.
Your hunger is for life, for life!

And you have understanding, and the power
To pierce the husk of words; to take an hour
Hot from the crisis of a soul
And live it in another, and so grow
Greater by each of us who only know
A part—and you the whole.

O friend, my friend, it's good to feel you there,
A solvent for all small hypocrisies,
A white and steady flare
That beacons over such confusing seas
To bring me truth.
It's good to know that youth
And eyes and lips are only half the tie;
That, though all listening peoples claim you now,
Your spirit still
Holds some small emptiness that I,
And only I, can fill.

So take my homage, friend, with all the rest.
It will not hurt you—you are much too wise—
And ride the world, and battle at the crest,
As at the ebb, with lies.
Yet if you weary sometimes of the praise
And greatness palls a little in the dusk,
I shall be waiting as in other days.
Then you can strip your world-ways like a husk,
And friendship will make wide her wicket gate
On twilit gardens, sweet and intimate,
And we will talk of simple homely things,
Of flowers, of laughter, of the flash of wings. . .

## To My Mad Love

O madder than the great mad wind
That skims the singing sky,
When all the earth is taut with spring,
And every joyous frolic thing
Whirls laughing by!

O madder than the great round sun,
And than the glad green sea
That leaps to feel herself caressed,
Panting beneath the sun-god's breast
In ecstasy.

O mad as only gods are mad
Who know the sting of pain,
And yet ride over it like chaff,
Who trample it with joy, and laugh,
And laugh again.

O mad with a creator's joy
Of life and love set free,
Oh, you have lit the earth with fire
And waked in all her young desire
The spring in me!

## Imprisoned

I have walked always in a veil.
A clinging shroud encircles me,
Steel-strong, yet yielding, and too frail
For any eye to see.

No blow can rend it, and no knife
Can slash the subtle formless thing.
It shuts me in with my own life
Past hope or questioning.

If I reach out my hand to touch
Some meeting hand of god or man,
The veil gives backward just so much
As my arm's length can span.

I cannot hope to loose its hold
Till I am free of transient suns.
I grow more separate in its folds
With every year that runs.

And yet I cannot be content.
I cry out like a lonely child;
I struggle, but my strength is spent;
I am not reconciled.

Oh, brother, whom I cannot reach,
Not willingly I pass you by!
My heart is clumsy, and my speech,
But, brother, hear my cry!

## The Dream Goes On

The work goes on, the dream goes on!
We are the tide-waves, nothing more;
Our separate lives beat and are gone
Upon the shore.

The dream goes on! Past peace, past war,
Past life or death, past fear or fate,
Mounts beauty like a virgin star
Inviolate.

## From a Hospital Bed

This is a house of many-fingered pain,
Swift fingers, pitiless, that probe and press;
A sullen house, where torture is and stress,
And where drugged nightmare dreams grow real again.
Here in the darkness shudder cries, that strain
Like living things, throbbing and powerless,
Against dead walls grown pale with weariness,
And dull, blank windows where the sick hours wane.

Yet here—begot by very violence
Of pain, that pain might sting itself, and heal—
The living spirit of compassion dwells
And ministers in fervent diligence
With keen strong hands; till I who lie here feel
That heaven has stooped and laid its lips to hell's.

## Parting After a Quarrel

You looked at me with eyes grown bright with pain
Like some trapped thing's. And then you moved your
    head
Slowly from side to side, as though the strain
Ached in your throat with anger and with dread.

And then you turned and left me, and I stood
With a queer sense of deadness over me,
And only wondered dully that you could
Fasten your trench-coat up so carefully

Till you were gone. Then all the air was thick
With my last words that seemed to leap and quiver.
And in my heart I heard the little click
Of a door that closes—quietly, forever.

## Gloria Mundi

In what dim, half-imagined place
Does the Titanic lie today,
Too deep for tide, too deep for spray,
In night and saltiness and space?

Oh, quiet must the sea-floor be!
And very still must be the gloom
Where in each well-appointed room
The splendor rots unto the sea.

Through crannies in the shattered decks
The sea-weed thrusts pale finger-tips,
And in the bottom's jagged rips
With ghostly hands it waves and becks.

The mirrors in the great saloons
Sleep darkly in their gilt and brass,
Save when the silent fishes pass
With eyes like phosphorescent moons.

On painted walls are slimy things;
And strange sea creatures, lithe and cool,
Spawn in the marble swimming pool
And shall—a thousand thousand springs.

For as it is, so it shall be,
Untouched of time till doom appears,
Too deep for days, too deep for years,
In the salt quiet of the sea.

## Transcontinental

The train spins forward endlessly.
Outside
The sunlit trees and the patient procreant fields
Flash past me and are gone.
Drab little houses pass me silently,
Colored without from the drab lives within.

I see them, and I see them not.
My heart
Half dwells behind me, lingering with lips new-lost,
And half leaps forward to the journey's end.
Only my body sits here listlessly,
Here where the sunlit trees
Flash past me and are gone.

## Dusk

The pathway of the setting sun
Flakes up the sea to westward;
My heart cries out, now day is done,
To you—to you—and restward.

The white gulls flit towards shore and hill
That flew this morning foamward,
But my heart circles, crying still,
And may not turn it homeward.

## The Tepid Hour

In such a tepid night as this
Strange formless sorrowings lie hid,
Like melancholy in a kiss,
Like what we dreamed in what we did,
In such a tepid night as this.

From out some shadowy depths of me
Vague longings struggle, dreamer-wise;
They stir and moan uneasily,
Then sleep again, too weak to rise
From out those shadowy depths of me.

Life holds me by so frail a thread
That scarce I feel the drag of it.
Alive I seem, and yet half dead.
But quick or dead I care no whit,
Life holds me by so frail a thread.

I would not snap the thread, and yet
Light as it is I grudge its hold.
'Twere broken with no more regret
Than lingers round a love grown old;
I would not snap the thread, and yet . .

## Lament of a Poetry Editor

Heigh-ho, how many songs they write,
The great ones and the small!
Although I sit from noon till night
I cannot read them all.

They write of most important things,
Of wisdom old and new.
But oh, the little words with wings—
They are so few—so few!

## Praise for Him

And if I find you beautiful, what then?
Shall I not take my pleasure in the line
Of your clean chiseled nostril, and the fine
Crisp curve your hair makes on your forehead? Men
Are plenty who are dull and dutiful.
I owe you thanks that you are beautiful.

And if your spirit's vividness is such
That with the swiftness of a flight of birds
Rises the covey of your colored words,
Where is the song shall praise you overmuch?
I hold no brief for pious lividness;
I thank you for your spirit's vividness.

And if your soul—"Is there a soul?" "Perhaps;
At least admit it as a way men speak."—
Your soul then, lonely as a mountain peak
And naked as a fawn, if it can lapse
Sheer outward from the rim of things I see,
Well! I'm still thankful for your liberty.

## Silence

Between us two a silence lies
Ringed all about with sound.
Beneath the crash of work-day cries,
Beneath night's whispering of sighs
It wraps me round.

It is more silent than the deep
Below the sounding sea;
More silent than the stars that keep
Lone watches where the world-winds sweep
Across eternity.

It folds me from the blatant day
And from the noisy street.
Remote and still I go my way,
Feeling, behind the fret and fray,
The heart of silence beat.

# Night-watch in the Life Saving Station

"Ten minutes late tonight!"
"I'm sorry, Cap.
Examinations are next week you know,
And that biology's a reg'lar trap.
Those tricky slides . . . and then I love it so.
I crammed too late. I'm sorry."
"Let it go.
But that's the trouble with this student crew,—
Late every one of you!
There's nothing to report. Good night."
"Good night—and thank you, Cap."

Already it is dusk, and in my sight
Skies and the sea are spread.
The west still tingles with the after-glow
Behind me, but before
The fragile air deepens to indigo
And the sea sighs, and nestles in its bed.
The long curved line of shore
Is strung with points of light, and more and more
The grinding sounds of labor cease;
The cup of day is full.
How beautiful is peace—
How beautiful! . . .

Far out across the dark and breathing sea
A single ship, a human point of light,
Trails through the growing night
Lone as a soul.

Its tiny flame, set in immensity,
Seems as remote, as separate from me
As pole from Arctic pole.

Yet suddenly, if the blown sea should rise,
Heedless of things afloat
Hurtling itself against the skies,
And from my throat
The cry should come, "A ship is in distress!"
Then soul would leap to soul across the waste,
And I should hear, below me in the mess,
Shouts, and the rush of feet, and the crisp sound
Of oil-skins donned in haste.
And on the beach
Man and the sea would grip. The vicious reach,
The hammer and rebound
Of the piled surf would beat him back to land.
But he would struggle up, and stand
To hurl himself again into the sea;
And there would be
Eyes stung with salt, blind cries across the night,
And straining muscles, and hard laboring breath,
And fear, and helplessness, and death—
Yes, even death perhaps,
Because of that lone light.
So are we knit. So man's new faith leaps free
In the old fight.

But the storm sleeps—and slowly from my sight
The spark drifts out; and on the sighing sea
Night broods, and beauty; little winds that cease;

All ageless things, all mystery,
And blue deep-driven peace.
So looked the bright bent moon when from the slime
The ape my father grew aware of time
And stood a man—to hurl across the dark
The yearning and the challenge and the spark,
Dumbly, as I tonight am dumb.
And so the sea has sighed
With ebb and tide
A million million years to come. . . .

Here on my height between the earth and sky
Watching, remote, the wheel of life go by,
Almost I can appraise
With final judgment these small human lives,
This homely, patient litany of days,
That wakes and strives
Beside the everlasting sea.
Here in the night the clinging veil wears thin,
The veil of self that hems me in;
Almost I feel a godhead grow in me,
The clanging spirit of old prophecy,
To hurl my soul,
My ringing human soul,
Forward along man's pathway to the goal;
To gather up in one fierce ecstasy
All threads, all knowledge and all mystery,
To know—and know—
So burst this little I
And, knowing, die

And be at peace.
Almost, almost—I see . . .

"What, you already, Mate? My watch is past?
I never knew the hours to go so fast.
I got to thinking—it's my last resort!
Good night, Mate.
No, there's nothing to report."

## At the Banquet

Above the wine and cigarettes,
Below the jest that flies,
I catch with half amused insistence,
Like throb of music in the distance,
Your eyes!

They knit the wine and jest together
In deeper harmonies;
With my own thoughts they interlace
Like some strange contrapuntal bass
Your eyes.

The words we speak say all—and nothing.
In them no mystery lies.
Only, between my soul and sense
Steal, half amused and half intense,
Your eyes. . . .

## Weariness

*I am so tired!*

A haze of heaviness is over me.
Voices come dully through the void;
And though I hardly understand
And my mind fumbles like a sightless thing
My tongue makes answer thickly.
All my world, the prick of all my being,
Dulls to this: only to rest, to rest,
And to be sunk miles deep
In inert flesh. . . .

*I am so tired.*

## Woodland Love Song

Hark to the woodland, the low thrilling hum of it,
Hark to the message that sings in the pine!
Love lies before us, the whole golden sum of it;
Come what may come of it,
Here you are mine!

Love of life, life of love, here we are part of it,
Here where the wood-odor moves me like wine.
Pure thrill of living, the joy and the smart of it,
Deep in the heart of it,
Here you are mine!

Yield me your lips, love, that make me the thrall of
you,
Yield me them glowing, half shy, half divine.
Love, how my being cries out at the call of you!
Oh, give me all of you,
Mine, all, all mine!

## On the Height

The foot-hills called us, green and sweet.
We dallied, but we might not stay;
And all day long we set our feet
In the wind's way.

We climbed with him the wandering trail
Up to the last keen, lonely height
Where snow-peaks clustered, sharp and frail,
Swimming in light.

Sheer on the edge of heaven we dwelt,
And laughed above the blue abyss,
While on my happy lips I felt
Your windy kiss.

You were the spirit of the height,
The breath of sun and air. . . .
A bird dipped wing, and, swift and white,
Peace brooded there.

## Three Spring Poems

In Imitation of the Japanese

I

In the sweet spring rain
The small fingers of the grass
Tender little yearning things,
Reach up towards the sky.
Do you think to find the sun?

II

It is cold tonight.
The last fold of winter's robe
Trails across the land;
Yet I see a soft green bud
Broidered on the hem of it.

III

Little cherry bud,
Hidden in your close brown leaves,
Are you truly there?
Or since spring has come to me
Do I only dream of you?

## To a West Indian Alligator

(Estimated age, 1957 years [1])

Greetings, my brother, strange and uncouth beast,
Flat-bellied, wrinkled, broad of nose!
You are not beautiful—and yet at least
Contentment spreads your scaly toes.

The keeper thwacks you and you grunt at me,
Two hundred pounds of sleepy spleen.
He tells me that your cranial cavity
Will just contain a lima bean.

How seems it, brother, you who are so old,
To lie and squint with curtained eye
At these ephemera, born in the cold,
These human things, so soon to die?

You were scarce grown, a paltry eighty years,
Too young to think of breeding yet,
When Christ the Nazarene loosed the salt tears
Which on man's cheeks today are wet.

Mohammed rose and died—you churned the mud
And watched your female laying eggs.
Columbus passed you—with an oozy thud
You scrambled sunward on your legs.

So now you doze at ease for all to view

[1] I cannot vouch for the science of this. It is "Alligator Joe's" estimate.

And bat a sleepy lid at me;
You eat a little every year or two
And count time in eternity.

So, brother, which is wiser of us twain
When words are said, and meals are past?
I think, and pass—you sleep, yet you remain,
And where shall be the end at last?

## To Sara Teasdale

From my life's outer orbit, where the night
That bounds my knowledge still is piercèd through
By far-off singing planets such as you,
Whose faint sweet voices come to me like light
In disembodied beauty, keen and bright—
From this far orbit to my nearer view
You came one day, grown tangible and true
And warm with sympathy and fair with sight.
Then I who still had loved your distant voice,
Your songs, shot through with beauty and with tears
And woven magic of the wistful years,
I felt the listless heart of me rejoice
And stir again, that had lain stunned so long,
Since I had you, yourself a living song.

## To Amy Lowell

who visits me in a hospital.

Like a fleet with bellying sails,
Like the great bulk of a sea-cliff with the staccato bark
of waves about it,
Like the tart tang of the sea breeze
Are you;
Filling the little room where I lie straitly on a white
island between pain and pain.

## Winter Rain

Winter now has come again;
All the gentle summer rain
Has grown chill, and stings like pain,
And it whispers of things slain,
Love of mine.

I had thought to bury love,
All the ways and wiles thereof
Buried deep and buried rough—
But it has not been enough,
Heart of mine.

Though I buried him so deep,
Tramped his grave and piled it steep,
Strewed with flowers the aching heap,
Yet it seems he cannot sleep,
Soul of mine.

And the drops of winter rain
In the grave where he is lain
Drip, and drip, and sting like pain;
Till my love grows live again,
Life of mine!

## Nuit Blanche

My soul is filled with huge, unfinished things,
The vast abortions of the world, tonight,
With monstrous crags, spewed upward to the light
By a sick, travailing earth; with headlong springs
That rush untimely to their burgeonings;
With rivers that flash downward from the height
Yearning to seaward, doomed to end their flight
In the slow choking that the desert brings.

And love is with me too, inchoate, dire,
Aping your features, like you—yet untrue,
Aborted, botched, a mockery of you.
It sears my yearning body with desire;
My very soul grows formless in its heat,
And in the whole world nothing is complete.

## A Song of Sailing

Peaceful and patient under the moon,
Hugging the hills, it has cuddled down,
Close by the sea where the strange winds croon,
Your little town.

You are at peace there under the hills,
You who have gathered the stars for me;
Strong are your roots, and the green sap fills
Yearly the tree.

Oh, but for me who am outward bound
Into the night and the sea's long quest,
Seeking the goal that is never found—
Where is there rest?

## After Love

Oh, I am restless, restless!
At its root
My life is withering that was so sound.

Once I knew singing. I have felt my throat
Ache with the sharp, unutterable cry,
And poured my melted being in a note
More pure, more free, more rapturous than I.

And peace I knew. My open hands have lain
On quiet sands that harbored all the sun.
Yea, my soul has grown fertile as the rain
And deep as dusk when wandering is done.

And I knew beauty. To my tunèd eyes
The east has shaken with the dawnlight thrills,
And the wild glory of the naked skies
Trembled to dusk along the western hills.

These I have known and brought them all to love.
But love is gone, and now
They have dropped from me like the fickle leaves,
While at its root
My life is withering that was so sound,
And I am restless, restless!

## The Steam Shovel

Beneath my window in a city street
A monster lairs, a creature huge and grim
And only half believed; the strength of him—
Steel strung and fit to meet
The strength of earth—
Is mighty as men's dreams that conquer force.
Steam belches from him. He is the new birth
Of old Behemoth, late sprung from the source
Whence Grendel sprang, and all the monster clan
Dead for an age, now born again of man.

The iron head
Set on a monstrous, jointed neck,
Glides here and there, lifts, settles on the red
Moist floor, with nose dropped in the dirt, at beck
Of some incredible control.
He snorts, and pauses couchant for a space,
Then slowly lifts; and tears the gaping hole
Yet deeper in earth's flank. A sudden race
Of loosened earth and pebbles trickles there
Like blood-drops in a wound.
But he, the monster, swings his load around
Weightless it seems as air. His mammoth jaw
Drops widely open with a rasping sound
And all the red earth vomits from his maw.

Oh, patient monster, born at man's decree,
A lap-dog dragon, eating from his hand
And doomed to fetch and carry at command,

Have you no longing ever to be free?
In warm electric days to run a-muck,
Ranging like some mad dinosaur,
Your fiery heart at war
With this strange world, the city's restless ruck,
Where all drab things that toil, save you alone,
Have life;
And you the semblance only—and the strife?
Do you not yearn to rip the roots of stone
Of these great piles men build
And hurl them down with shriek of shattered steel,
Scorning your own sure doom, so you may feel,
You too, the lust with which your sires killed?
Or is your soul in very deed so tame,
The blood of Grendel watered to a gruel,
That you are well content
With heart of flame
Thus placidly to chew your cud of fuel
And toil in peace for man's aggrandizement?

Poor helpless creature of a half grown god,
Blind of yourself and impotent!
At night
When your forerunners, sprung from quicker sod,
Ranged through primeval woods, hot on the scent,
Or waked the stars with amorous delight,
You stand, a soiled unwieldy mass of steel,
Black in the arc-light, modern as your name,
Dead and unsouled and trite;
Till I must feel
A quick creator's pity for your shame—

That man who made you and who gave so much
Yet cannot give the last transforming touch,
That with the work he cannot give the wage,
For day, no joy of night,
For toil, no ecstasy of primal rage.

## Mud

This road is a river of mud.
It sucks and gurgles and splashes, almost liquid on top, solidly tenacious underneath. With each step my boot sinks in, slips as I throw my weight forward, and comes out heavily with a sucking sound.
The soldiers driving the cars that pass me have mud in their hair, and their faces are white with drying mud.
Yet this is nothing. There is bottom here.

I am thinking of two Canadians who found a British soldier mired in Flanders.
He was in a hole in the road, sunk in to his arm-pits, stuck fast.
With their entrenching tools the two set out to dig him free. They dug fast, against time. But not fast enough.
Down the road a heavy gun strained forward to the front. If it stopped it would be mired beyond hope.
England needed the gun.
It didn't stop.

*Near Chiry,* 1917.

## Song for a Blind Man Who Could Not Go to War

*You who have no eyes to see*
*You were spared what shaketh me.*

Houses ribbed against the sky
Where the storm of steel went by;

Barbed wire rusting in the rain,
Still unwashed of human pain;

Children's eyes grown black with fear;
Grief too dead for sound or tear;

Earth with clotted death for yield;
Crows above a battlefield;

Brains like paint spilled on a wall,
And flesh that has no form at all;

And after nights when souls have gone
The lovely, heedless, heartless dawn.

*You who have no eyes to see*
*You were spared what shaketh me.*

*Paris,* 1918.

# Deserted Battlefield

Here, on the gentle slope of hill, in this great space, beneath this windy sky, men have lain down to sleep in No Man's Land, and fallen bit by bit away, and sunk, in sun and rain, close, closer to the earth; and come at last to be one with the earth, for ever;
And so have come to peace, where all roads end, nor any cry can come.

Ah, yes! But there is pain! But there is pain.
My shuddering spirit breaks itself on pain.
There are these pointed stakes, this twisted wire, these barbed and saw-toothed traps for flesh!
Here men have hung, their living bodies shattered,—hung, and watched the sun, and cringed with little cries, and called on God,.
And thirst has twisted in them like a blade.

We do not come so easily to death. He is a lover we must search for long, and woo with agony, and clasp with pain,
A lover hard to please—who yet at last clips down upon us, merciful, and stops our mouth with peace, and puts to rest the quick, caged throbbing of our brain.
Death we can love at last.

But, O great God, what shall we do with pain?

*Near Ville,* 1917.

# Translations

## and Renderings into English Verse

## Since I Have Set My Lips

From the French of Victor Hugo

Since I have set my lips to your exhaustless bowl,
Since in your cooling hands my pallid forehead lay,
Since I have breathed at times the sweet breath of
your soul,
Like perfume in the shadows, too delicate for day—

Since I have heard you say, yearning toward me the
while,
Words where the heart lies hid, mysterious and wise,
Since I have seen you weep, since I have seen you smile,
Your lips on my lips and your eyes on my eyes—

Since I have felt, agleam on my enchanted head,
A ray from your far star, veiled always to my gaze,
Since on my life's dark wave a rose-leaf has been shed,
A petal dropped to me from roses of your days—

Now can I truly say to the swift-running years:
Pass on! Pass on in vain; my love is not afraid.
You sluggards, get you gone, in faded flowers and
tears!
In my safe heart I hide a flower you cannot fade.

Against my spirit's urn your mighty pinion dashes,
Yet nothing shall you spill of joy that I possess;
My soul has more of fire than you can have of ashes,
My heart has more of love than you forgetfulness!

## Autumn Song

From the French of Paul Verlaine

The long-drawn sobs
That autumn throbs
On strings a-weary,
Wound my heart
With languid smart,
Endless, dreary . . .

All pallid then,
Half stifled, when
Strikes the hour,
I call to mind
Sweet years behind,
And tears shower.

Ill winds that shift
Set me a-drift,
Scudding, flying,
Now there, now here,
Like to the sere
Leaf dying.

# The Sail

From the Russian of Mihail Yuryevich Lermontov

A far sail brightens, solitary,
The thin, blue distance of the sea.
What question does its taut heart carry?
What does it seek? What does it flee?

The storm shrieks wild, the blown sea lurches,
The bending mast creaks in the wind.
Alas! It finds, though still it searches,
No happiness before, behind. . . .

Below it, streams of the sea's blue wonder,
Above it, sun, and the clouds' white fleece.
But it, impetuous, seeks the thunder,
As though in the thunder there were peace.

## Sonnet

From the old Spanish of Fray Luis da Leon (1529–1591)

Now with the dawn she who is all my light
From sleep arises; now her lustrous hair
In coilèd knot she binds; and now her fair
Young breast and throat with gold she has bedight.
Now towards the heaven, with purity made bright
Her hands and eyes she raises, and a prayer
Of pity for my anguish trembles there.
And now she sings as grieving angel might.

Thus say I, and upheld by this dear dream
Before my eyes I seem to see her so.
And loving, very humble, I adore.
But later, on my self-tricked soul the gleam
Of truth descends. My destiny I know
And loose the flood-gates that my tears may pour.

# Contemporary Japanese Poems

(Rendered into English verse from
the literal translations of
Professor O. Yoshida in Tokio)

## On the Grass

After Rofu Miki ("Rural Vision," 1915)

I laid myself down on the grasses;
Dark grew the mountains and the passes.

An echo broke the autumn weather.
Dead trees and my flesh shook together.

The leaves were scattered. They seemed trying
To climb the sky as they were dying.

## The Heart of a Woman of Thirty

After Mrs. Akiko Yosano ("Dance Garments," 1916)

The heart of a woman of thirty
Is a measure of fire,
Having neither shade, nor smoke,
Nor sound.
It is a round sacred sun
In the sky at evening;
Silently,
Penetratingly,
It burns—burns.

## Songs

After Isamo Yoshii
(From Tosei Hashida's "Anthology of Modern Famous Poems," 1916)

I

Kichiya, who had been long ill, came out to the edge of the River Kamogawa and bent to look at the rushes.

II

Because one said to me:
"Beautiful, beautiful is the night! We shall never sleep tonight,"
Hardly can I forget one night at Uji.

## The Orphan

After Hakushu Kitahara

On a hill, in the glow of the evening,
She is weeping—and singing *Rappabushi.*[1]

In the midst of the glow of the evening
The peddler is dangling his puppet,
Clacking his tongue and his thin bronze fingers.
By wire and by note the doll climbs upward
And its feet of paper quiver.

On a hill, in the glow of the evening,
Hopelessly she is singing *Rappabushi.*
Weeps the flute, or is the puppet weeping?
Infinitely sorrowful drips the tune.
By wire and by note the doll climbs upward
And its feet of paper quiver.

O pitiful slave of Karma!
You shall be cold tonight, little orphan,
And passing bitter for your warm lost lover,
And that the rasping peddler beats you.
By wire and by note the doll climbs upward
And its feet of paper quiver.

On a hill, in the glow of the evening
*Rappabushi* dies in the twilight.

[1] *Rappabushi* (accented on the second syllable), meaning "trumpet note," is the title of a popular song.

## The Cup of Darkness

After Homei Iwano (Volume of the same name, 1908)

Like a lost jewel is my dream.
Though when I awake I search hungrily for it, alas,
I find it not.

The glow and the gleam are gone.
Only a hand remains, a hand which I stretch forth in
the darkness.

My joints relax; my strength runs out of them.
Even my love and my hope are half a dream.

When I open my eyes the sliding groove of darkness is
over me,
And strange torn visions wander there.

Devil! Rasetsu! Yasha's head!
What spirits cast these fevered shapes over me?

I am locked in the prison of death;
My flesh and my soul are burning.

Though the terror and menace of unseen fire and water
Are darkly over me,

Yet my life laughs like the foam of *saké*
And the sweet scent of mirth leads me into slumber.

The cup of darkness holds the darkness.
I sink in the fathomless night,

Where from dream to sliding dream
I shall glide forever . . .

Thanks are due to the editors of the following magazines for permission to reprint many of the poems in this volume: *Poetry, The Century, The Dial, Smart Set, The Masses, Everybody's, Reedy's Mirror, The Little Review, The Texas Review, The Poetry Review, The Cosmopolitan, The Stratford Journal, The Woman's Home Companion, The Chicago Daily News, The Chicago Evening Post.*

CPSIA information can be obtained
at www.ICGtesting.com
Printed in the USA
BVHW042053220920
589430BV00006B/484